T0209360

THE IDENTITY PROJECT

EZRA ROBINSON

WESTBOW
P R E S S®
A DIVISION OF THOMAS NELSON
& ZONDERVAN

WestBow Press books may be ordered through booksellers or by contacting:

WestBow Press
A Division of Thomas Nelson & Zondervan
1663 Liberty Drive
Bloomington, IN 47403
www.westbowpress.com
844-714-3454

ISBN: 979-8-3850-0482-9 (sc)
ISBN: 979-8-3850-0483-6 (e)

Library of Congress Control Number: 2023914933

Print information available on the last page.

WestBow Press rev. date: 8/24/2023

Introduction

Wake Up (06:40–7:53)

We live in a world where we are constantly bombarded with information. What's in, what's out, and what's expected of us, to fit in, constantly changes and demands our undivided attention. In other words, the world is relentlessly telling us who we should be, and what that looks like, every day of our lives.

"It's estimated that an American adult makes over thirty five thousand decisions a day"(Sollisch, Jim. "The cure for decision fatigue." Wall Street Journal 10 (2016)). Many of these decisions are a result of what we have been given in the form of an advertisement, regardless of our awareness of that fact. Ironically, we are more susceptible to advertising when we don't realize that it is happening to us (Tobey, "Advertising Works. Don't Believe Me? Then You Are My Favorite Demographic." https://medium.com/@dahanese/advertising-works-don-t-believe-me-then-you-are-my-favorite-demographic-ebf6b1f2541a). For example, if I bump into you and knock the coffee out of your hands without saying excuse me or turning around to acknowledge what happened, a message has been sent. Specifically, I have communicated, without words, that you are not important. Think about how scary this is as we are on the receiving end of countless 'advertisements.' Every. Single. Day.

I have had the opportunity to interview people with roots in different parts of the world. What each interview revealed was that each culture has a way of advertising its own brand of identity in various ways. It is almost as if there is safety in just belonging to a group without necessarily questioning its values. During one interview, an individual noted that they felt a sense of warmth and belonging being a part of their cultural group because of all the communal gatherings though he could not speak the language. We are wired to belong even if that means not living as who we are meant to be.

As believers, we live in the world and often struggle with insecurities as a part of having a fallen human nature. Being bombarded with identity-loaded information that does not reflect who we are in Christ amplifies that struggle. Rarely do we peel back every layer of the onion to understand why we don't have the confidence in Christ that He desires for us. Famous explanations heard from the pulpit include but are not limited to "we have a sin nature," "we need to pray more," and "as the people of God, we need to be content." These are all true but do not address practical ways to combat and understand what is taking place. It is equivalent to a doctor telling a patient they need to get medicine because they are sick without addressing the specific sickness or what type of medication they should take.

I spent a good portion of my adult life in abusive environments and relationships because deep down in my soul, I wanted to belong. There was something about being in a community that caused me to believe that sacrificing my identity and self-worth was worth being surrounded by people who said they loved me. However, God taught me a valuable lesson; evil surrounds people too and speaks the same words. Evil takes an essential human need and uses it to ensnare people in a cycle of forgetfulness that is hard to break free from. It was not until I started to discover who I was in Christ, and what that truly meant, that I began to understand that I already belonged. When I understood that I already had my belonging in Christ, I wasn't afraid of letting go and allowing Him to lead me to the environment and people He intended for me.

This nine-week study equips believers to identify the lies of the enemy we get from our society, the people in our lives (past, present, and future), and ourselves. It then equips us to understand who we are in Christ so we can name every lie, counter it with the truth of God's Word and find our true sense of belonging in Him above all.

For this study, we will be using the first *Matrix* film. The reason we use the *Matrix* film is that the visuals in cinematic storytelling are extremely powerful. This film's story closely identifies with the battles we face as believers in a false world. In *The Matrix*, Neo and his team must fight against their enemies in the context of a false world, called the Matrix, while their bodies are in the real world. However, what happens to them in the Matrix affects their bodies in the real world. As believers, we know that we do not wrestle against flesh and blood (Eph. 6), but what we do in this flesh still has spiritual consequences and vice versa. Going through the film and highlighting various clips will help us to see how our lives are not as different as we may think.

How it works:
- This study is broken up into three different phases.
- Each week, the group/individual will write down their answers and discuss with their group (if applicable) after watching the time stamped clip for the week. For example, the individual or group will watch and discuss the introductory one minute and thirteen seconds clip which starts at the six minutes and forty seconds mark of the movie and ends at the seven minutes and fifty-three

seconds mark during the first week. The introduction and first phase begin in Week 1.

- Each week is an opportunity for the reader to watch the week's clip and draw out how the symbolism reflects a part of their journey.
- There will be a lie section in the notes for each week where they write down the lies they are tempted to believe or act on according to that week's subject. Homework will be to find verses to renounce each lie.
- In the final week, each person will print out and laminate a list of "I am" statements according to their notes and bring them to class to share. They should post this list on a wall and/or save it in their smart phone or computer.

Phase 1

Understand the Matrix_
(11:30–11:59)

Week 1

What is identity and how does it influence your everyday life? Begin to reflect on why (Discuss the video clip with your group or reflect on it individually at home. How does the clip tie in with the question for the week?)

Take five minutes to write down your answer.

What lies do you believe related to this week's topic?

_____

_____

_____

_____

_____

_____

_____

_____

_____

_____

_____

_____

_____

_____

What does God's Word say?

_____

_____

_____

_____

_____

_____

_____

_____

_____

_____

_____

_____

_____

_____

_____

Phase 2

Escape the Matrix
(25:11–29:50)

(Watch the video clip each week during this phase.)

Week 2

What does society communicate about you? What false truth is being communicated? (Discuss the video clip with your group or reflect on it individually at home. How does the clip tie in with the question for the week?)

Take five minutes to write down your answer.

What lies do you believe related to this week's topic?

_____

_____

_____

_____

_____

_____

_____

_____

_____

_____

_____

_____

_____

What does God's Word say?

_____

_____

_____

_____

_____

_____

_____

_____

_____

_____

_____

_____

_____

_____

Week 3

What does your job communicate about you? Think about how you feel compared to others who have different jobs (Discuss the video clip with your group or reflect on it individually at home. How does the clip tie in with the question for the week?)

Take five minutes to write down your answer:

What lies do you believe related to this week's topic?

_____

_____

_____

_____

_____

_____

_____

_____

_____

_____

_____

_____

_____

_____

What does God's Word say?

_____

_____

_____

_____

_____

_____

_____

_____

_____

_____

_____

_____

_____

_____

Week 4

What do your co-workers communicate about you? Think about how your co-workers treat you in addition to what they may say (Discuss the video clip with your group or reflect on it individually at home. How does the clip tie in with the question for the week?)

Take five minutes to write down your answer.

What lies do you believe related to this week's topic?

_____

_____

_____

_____

_____

_____

_____

_____

_____

_____

_____

_____

_____

What does God's Word say?

_____

_____

_____

_____

_____

_____

_____

_____

_____

_____

_____

_____

_____

_____

_____

_____

Week 5

What do professional advertisements communicate about you? Think about what ads on the internet and television are trying to communicate about you (Discuss the video clip with your group or reflect on it individually at home. How does the clip tie in with the question for the week?)

Take five minutes to write down your answer.

What lies do you believe related to this week's topic?

_____

_____

_____

_____

_____

_____

_____

_____

_____

_____

_____

_____

_____

_____

What does God's Word say?

_____

_____

_____

_____

_____

_____

_____

_____

_____

_____

_____

_____

_____

_____

_____

Week 6

What do your peers communicate about you? Think about words and actions (Discuss the video clip with your group or reflect on it individually at home. How does the clip tie in with the question for the week?)

Take five minutes to write down your answer.

What lies do you believe related to this week's topic?

_____

_____

_____

_____

_____

_____

_____

_____

_____

_____

_____

_____

_____

_____

What does God's Word say?

_____

_____

_____

_____

_____

_____

_____

_____

_____

_____

_____

_____

_____

_____

_____

Week 7

What do your parents and role models communicate about you? Think about words and actions (Discuss the video clip with your group or reflect on it individually at home. How does the clip tie in with the question for the week?)

Take five minutes to write down your answer.

What lies do you believe related to this week's topic?

_____

_____

_____

_____

_____

_____

_____

_____

_____

_____

_____

_____

_____

_____

_____

What does God's Word say?

_____

_____

_____

_____

_____

_____

_____

_____

_____

_____

_____

_____

_____

_____

Phase 3

Break Free from the Influence of the Matrix (2:01:37–2:06:48)

Week 8

What does the Source of Truth communicate about you? Think about what your Heavenly Father communicates about you in His Word (Discuss the video clip with your group or reflect on it individually at home. How does the clip tie in with the question for the week?)

Take five minutes to write down your answer.

What lies do you believe related to this week's topic?

_____

_____

_____

_____

_____

_____

_____

_____

_____

_____

_____

_____

_____

What does God's Word say?

_____

_____

_____

_____

_____

_____

_____

_____

_____

_____

_____

_____

_____

_____

Week 8 Reminder: Compile a list of "I am" statements with scripture references based on notes taken throughout the study. Laminate this and bring it to class for week 9.

Week 9

Who are you?

Each person will take turns sharing their "I am" statements and any other part of their journey they feel led to share.

Pick an accountability partner from the group or a strong believer to meet with on a regular basis. Identity is a topic that should be covered each time the two meet. One of the greatest blessings I have ever had was a friend named James, whom I met at a house church in Phnom Penh, Cambodia. There was never a Sunday that went by where he did not challenge me to live in my identity in Christ. My hope and prayer for each person who has finished this study is that we will continue to do the work of remembering who we are in Christ and living in the truth of whom He has called us to be.

Additional Resources:

Want more? Check out the-identity-project.org, where Ezra posts weekly using scripture and storytelling through film to challenge both himself and others to live in their identity in Christ. He uses a variety of genres to help us see what we have been called to. Come join the community!

Printed in the United States
by Baker & Taylor Publisher Services